AS Economics & Business Studies
UNITS 2&3

Edexcel
Nuffield

Module 3: Change
Portfolio

Andrew Ashwin

This guide is dedicated to Alwyn Brace (an inspirational teacher), Nancy Wall (for her encouragement) and Sue, Alex and Jonathan (for being there).

Philip Allan Updates
Market Place
Deddington
Oxfordshire
OX15 0SE

Orders
Bookpoint Ltd, 130 Milton Park, Abingdon, Oxfordshire, OX14 4SB
tel: 01235 827720
fax: 01235 400454
e-mail: uk.orders@bookpoint.co.uk
Lines are open 9.00 a.m.–5.00 p.m., Monday to Saturday, with a 24-hour message answering service. You can also order through the Philip Allan Updates website:
www.philipallan.co.uk

© Philip Allan Updates 2006

ISBN-13: 978-1-84489-563-2
ISBN-10: 1-84489-563-7

In all cases we have attempted to trace and credit copyright owners of material used.

This guide has been written specifically to support students preparing for the Edexcel (Nuffield) AS Economics and Business Studies Unit 2 examination and Unit 3 portfolio. The content has been neither approved nor endorsed by Edexcel and remains the sole responsibility of the author.

Printed by MPG Books, Bodmin

Environmental information
The paper on which this title is printed is sourced from managed, sustainable forests.

Contents

Introduction

Aims 4

The Nuffield course 4

How to use this guide 4

Exam format 5

Assessment objectives 5

A 4-week structured revision plan 7

Planning your portfolio: general points 8

Tackling the portfolio 9

■ ■ ■

Content Guidance

About this section 16

What are the challenges?

How do markets change? 17

Rivalry or collaboration? 20

Will total output change? 24

Unemployment or inflation? 31

Why trade? 34

Which way forward?

Why are business plans important? 37

What makes markets grow? 39

What makes an economy grow? 41

Can we control the economy? 42

What should governments spend? 45

■ ■ ■

Questions and Answers

About this section 48

Section A 49

Section B 53

Section C 57

Introduction

Aims

The aim of this guide is to prepare you for Units 2 and 3 of the Edexcel (Nuffield) Advanced Subsidiary (AS) GCE examination in economics and business studies. It summarises the content covered in Module 3 and suggests approaches to the Unit 2 exam and the Unit 3 portfolio.

Module 3 focuses on the concept of change. Businesses are faced with change continually, much of which is triggered by economic events. The reasons for change and the ways in which businesses deal with it are covered in two sections:

(1) **Change 1: What are the challenges?** This section builds on material from Modules 1 and 2, looking first at why markets change and introducing the concept of the macroeconomy. Changes in the macroeconomy and issues such as unemployment, economic growth and exchange rates are also covered.

(2) **Change 2: Which way forward?** This section focuses on ways in which businesses can respond to change. It explores some of the causes of growth in both micro- and macro-markets that businesses have to factor into their planning. Government financial planning is also considered in terms of its effect on businesses.

The Nuffield course

It is important that you bear in mind throughout this unit the nature of the Nuffield course. The Nuffield approach aims to encourage you to investigate in your studies by asking a series of questions. Your goal is to develop a toolkit of skills that you can use in your investigations. Selecting the right tool to tackle a question or problem is a crucial part of your development as a good Nuffield student. These tools include knowing when to apply your knowledge, how to break down issues into manageable chunks and when and how to make appropriate judgements.

Active learning techniques can help you to develop these skills: getting involved in the subject and reading around the topic areas. You should try to get experience of making decisions (right or wrong) and understand what their implications are. Remember that there is nothing wrong with making mistakes — this is an important and essential part of the learning process. If you understand why you have made a mistake, you will learn how to avoid repeating it next time.

How to use this guide

This guide provides you with the insights and strategies needed to achieve a good grade. As with any guide, its value depends on how you use it. If you take on board the advice given and, most importantly, try to put it into practice, you will give yourself a good chance of getting the grade you want.

It is important that you understand that simply reading this guide will not necessarily give you the skills and knowledge needed to get a high grade. Study at AS is about developing certain skills and this can be achieved only through practice — through trying and making mistakes.

This introduction presents some of the key aspects of preparing your portfolio for Unit 3. You have to submit two pieces of portfolio work, which account for 30% of the weighting for the AS assessment (and 15% of the A-level).

The Content Guidance section presents an overview of the topics in Module 3. This material is tested in the Unit 2 exam, along with the content from Module 2 (Efficiency). The Question and Answer section has examples of questions which are typical of those you will meet in the examination. It gives student answers covering different qualities of response with accompanying comments from an examiner's perspective. These comments will help you to see what the examiner is looking for in an answer and how you can avoid making some common mistakes.

Exam format

Unit 2 accounts for 40% of the weighting for the AS examination (and 20% of the A-level). The exam is a written paper in which you have to answer:
- a series of structured questions in section A
- one question from a choice of two in section B
- one question from a choice of two in section C

You have 1 hour and 45 minutes to complete the three sections. Remember that the Unit 2 exam assesses the material covered in both Module 2 (Efficiency) and Module 3 (Change). The layout of the Unit 2 examination was changed in 2005, so it is important to familiarise yourself with the new format.

Assessment objectives

Your answers to exam questions and your portfolio work are judged against four assessment objectives (AOs). Understanding the assessment objectives and recognising what is being assessed in a question or in your portfolio pieces are important if you are to maximise your chances of getting a good grade. Many students ignore the assessment objectives and, as a result, fail to do themselves justice. After each set of examinations, Edexcel publishes examiners' reports. You are strongly advised to read these reports and act on the advice and warnings that the examiners give.

Paying attention to command words will help you to understand which assessment objectives are being targeted in a question. Further information on command words is provided later in this section.

In Unit 3 (the portfolio) the assessment objectives are weighted at different proportions, as shown in the table on p. 6.

Objective	Assessment objectives	Weighting
AO1	**Knowledge and understanding:** demonstrate knowledge and understanding of specified content.	25%
AO2	**Application:** apply knowledge and critical understanding to problems and issues arising from both familiar and unfamiliar situations.	25%
AO3	**Analysis:** analyse problems, issues and situations.	25%
AO4	**Evaluation:** evaluate and assess information, distinguish between fact and opinion and make reasoned judgements.	25%

Note that the weighting of the assessment objectives for the Unit 3 portfolio work differs from that for the Unit 1 and 2 exams. Greater emphasis is placed on the higher-order skills of analysis (AO3) and evaluation (AO4) in Unit 3.

The Unit 1 and 2 guides in this series describe how you can meet these assessment objectives. You will find details of how the assessment objectives are relevant to your portfolio later in this guide.

Summary of assessment objectives

Keeping the assessment objectives in mind at all times is important if you want to ensure that you get a good grade for your portfolio. Many students make the common error in their portfolio work of relying on content and description instead of focusing on analysis and evaluation.

The table below gives an outline of some of the key command words used in exam questions. The meanings of these words are listed, together with the assessment objectives that they target.

Command word	Meaning
Analyse	Requires you to break down a problem/issue into smaller parts, possibly looking for causes, consequences, reasons etc. What counts is not the quantity of factors identified but the quality of the development. (AO3)
Consider	Requires you to break down an issue into manageable parts (analysis) — generally involves consideration of different perspectives. (AO3)
Describe	Requires some development of a point made. May involve 'telling a story' to illustrate what is happening. (AO1/AO2)
Discuss	A requirement to analyse and to offer some form of judgement or appreciation of different viewpoints. (AO3/AO4)
Evaluate/assess	Requires some judgement. Answers should incorporate some analysis but the emphasis is on supported judgement — you should consider the 'it depends' rule. (AO4)
Examine	Requires some development of points and some analysis — some balance may need to be offered, i.e. seeing different aspects of the problem or different perspectives on the problem. (AO3/AO4)

introduction

Command word	Meaning
Explain	To make something plain or comprehensible, to offer some development of a point. (all four AOs)
Identify	Merely point out — little or no development required — a list would suffice. (mostly AO1)
List	No development needed — knowledge recall. (AO1)
What...?	Tends to focus on knowledge recall — often linked with the requirement of an example to demonstrate some application. (AO1/AO2)

A 4-week structured revision plan

The following table is a suggested plan for revision of the content in Module 3 in the 4 weeks before the Unit 2 exam, taking up to 5 hours each week. This does not mean that you should start your revision only 4 weeks before the exam — the plan is an outline of how to focus your attention in that final period. Remember that you have other subjects to revise, as well as extra work from your teachers, so it is important to try to keep a balance between the different parts of your study.

Hours	Week 1	Week 2	Week 3	Week 4
1st	Factors causing changes in markets.	Causes and consequences of inflation and unemployment.	Business plans, sources of finance and cash flow.	Economic growth and economic policy.
2nd	Competitive strategies and mergers.	Exchange rates.	Developing new products and the product life cycle.	Public spending.
3rd	Aggregate demand and supply.	Do two timed practice questions from section B of a past exam paper.	Marketing strategies.	Do one timed question from section C of a past exam paper and use the mark scheme to check your answers.
4th	Do an open-book practice question from section A of a past exam paper.	Use a published mark scheme (available from Edexcel or your school or college) to work through your answer — mark your own work for one of the questions.	Do one open-book question from section C of a past exam paper.	Do two questions from section C of a past exam paper under timed conditions.

Hours	Week 1	Week 2	Week 3	Week 4
5th	Do a second open-book practice question from section A of a past exam paper.	Use the mark scheme to assess the second question you answered.	Use the mark scheme to check your answers to the question. Focus on how the higher-order skills are assessed. Review your answer in the light of the mark scheme. Redo those parts where you identified weaknesses.	Use a mark scheme to check your answers to the practice questions. Review and rewrite your response in light of the weaknesses identified.

When following this revision plan, ensure that you leave gaps between the hours that you spend doing a task. For example, attempt a practice question on one day and then check it through on another. This will help you to focus on what you have written — it is surprising what you notice after a gap.

Planning your portfolio: general points

Your school has to submit your portfolio work around mid-May. You have to offer two pieces, each of 1,250 words in length. One piece should cover material studied in Module 1 and the other should be based on topics from Modules 2 or 3.

Working on your portfolio requires planning and careful time management. The idea behind the portfolio is that you complete a range of short tasks during your studies and build a collection of work that shows how you have progressed. The Nuffield course develops your skills of investigation and enquiry, which you can demonstrate through your portfolio work.

Although schools differ in their approaches to the portfolio, this guide offers some general advice on planning your work.

- **Frame your portfolio around a question.** The question should allow you to meet all the assessment objectives. Avoid questions such as 'How do exchange rates affect a company?' This could lead you to describe exchange rates rather than analyse or assess the impact of exchange rates. This question could be better phrased as 'Are exchange rates the most significant factor affecting a company's performance?' — this would allow you to evaluate the effects of exchange rates compared with those of other factors.
- **Plan your portfolio work carefully.** Research can take much longer than you think. If you need to write to companies for information, you should allow at least 3 weeks for a reply.
- **Make the work manageable.** Avoid grand titles that sound interesting but are too broad or complex. For example, the question 'Can global warming be solved?' is too vague and complicated to be tackled at AS.

- **Do not copy chunks of information from the internet.** This is cheating. If you want to refer to information you have found on the web, it must be acknowledged and referenced appropriately.
- **Use a range of resources to demonstrate your research and investigation skills.** Include a bibliography and a list of web addresses that give details of your sources of information.
- **Include an appendix in your work.** The appendix should contain details of your information sources (bibliography and list of web addresses), support material such as results of a primary investigation, and notes on facts, content and knowledge that you have gathered during your investigation.
- **Stick to the word limit.** You must write no more than 1,250 words for each portfolio piece (approximately 3 sides of typed A4 paper). Therefore, the work you submit for assessment should be just the answer to your question, not including, for example, pages of pie charts from your survey. These charts and other results can be included in the appendix. Remember that you are being marked against all the assessment objectives, including analysis and evaluation.

Tackling the portfolio

General points
- Each piece of work is referred to as an 'investigation'. Your collection of investigations makes up the portfolio. You choose two pieces to be submitted for assessment.
- Try to select a topic that interests you. You will find that many issues have economic and business applications. The only requirement is that the topic is relevant to the appropriate module.
- You can use primary or secondary sources of information in your investigation. A primary source is not essential for each investigation.
- One of the aims of the portfolio is to develop wider skills that may not be assessed by a written examination. Using your initiative and being creative and imaginative are parts of the learning process you undergo as an A-level student.
- Where possible, use a topical issue as the subject for your investigation — information should be available more readily.
- Try to generate your own questions for your investigations. Some schools adopt a different approach to portfolio work, but the idea behind the Nuffield course is that you take responsibility for your work — this includes deciding on the titles of your investigations.
- Make sure that your question is appropriate — not too broad or too narrow — and that it allows you to demonstrate the full range of assessment objectives.
- You may find that local issues are more accessible and manageable than national or international issues, which can be too broad.
- Remember to record where your information comes from. If you are using the internet, copy and paste the web address (URL) as a reminder of the source and note the date when you accessed the website. Make sure you add the sources to your list of websites.

- Include a full bibliography of your information sources, such as textbooks, newspapers, television interviews or programmes.
- Provide an appendix that contains evidence you have collected in support of your investigation — for example, your bibliography and list of web addresses, newspaper cuttings, copies of survey questionnaires, results of surveys, data etc. The appendix is not included in the word count.
- Although you should try not to exceed the 1,250 word limit, it is usually acceptable to write approximately 100–200 words more. However, if your word count is even greater, you are unlikely to get the highest marks for AO3, which involves selection and organisation of material.
- Do not copy chunks of information from the internet or any other source without referencing it. It is acceptable to quote material or comments as part of your work to support your argument, but the sources must be acknowledged properly. Further details on referencing are given below.
- For each submitted piece, include a cover sheet that offers a brief description of the investigation in one paragraph. Outline what you discovered and what your conclusions are. Writing the summary for the cover sheet should help you to clarify your thinking and argument and is not included in the 1,250 word count.
- Make use of the Nuffield toolkit in your investigation. Ensure that you use appropriate concepts, methods, theories and ideas in analysing and evaluating your investigation.
- Remember that one of your submitted pieces has to be related to Module 1 (Objectives) and the other to Module 2 (Efficiency) or Module 3 (Change).
- If you work in a group, ensure that your piece is different and that you can stamp your own individuality on it.

Referencing work

There is growing concern over the extent of plagiarism (copying) and cutting and pasting of information in coursework in both schools and universities. There is nothing wrong in using information gathered by someone else, but attempting to pass it off as your own work is strictly prohibited. This is cheating and can lead to disqualification from the exam.

Neither your teacher (your internal assessor) nor the moderator wants to read someone else's work. They want to find out what *you* think and see which skills *you* can demonstrate. Most teachers know their students well enough to detect copying. Often the language used is different and there are obvious errors in the text — copying is more noticeable than you may think.

In using textbooks, the internet and other sources to gather information, you may come across quotations that summarise a point you want to make or text that outlines a topic perfectly. If you want to use this information exactly as it is, it may be better placed in the appendix, especially if it is long. However, if you use original material from another source in the main part of your investigation, it must be referenced. Below are some examples of how to acknowledge sources of information:

- **Referencing a textbook in the bibliography** — quote the author, the date of publication, the title and the publisher:
  Wales, J., Wall, N. and Barnes, S. (2000) *Nuffield Economics and Business Students' Book*, Longman
- **Referencing a newspaper article** — give the author, article title, newspaper title and date:
  Michael Glackin, 'Economics daily report', *City A.M.*, 17 February 2006
- **Referencing a website** — give the title, web address, date of the article (if appropriate) and the date that you accessed the site:
  'The London Olympic Bid: Money well spent?',
  www.bized.ac.uk/current/mind/2004_5/221104.htm
  22 November 2004, accessed 14 February 2006
- **Referencing a data source** — Office for National Statistics from
  www.statistics.gov.uk/cci/nugget.asp?id=19

Suggested questions

Below are some suggestions of questions that you could tackle in your investigations. They are meant only to give you an idea of the types of questions or titles that are acceptable — they have *not* been approved by Edexcel or by any school or examiner.

The questions cover a range of topics and demonstrate how current issues can be used for investigations. The first examples are questions that may *not* be appropriate. A brief explanation is offered as to why this is the case and the question is rephrased to make it more acceptable. The aim is to help you appreciate the importance of selecting the right question that allows you to address all the assessment objectives.

- **Identify the stakeholders of the Body Shop and discuss its accountability to each.** This title is not a question and is too descriptive, making it difficult for you to show any evaluation skills.
  Alternative: Who is the most important stakeholder to the Body Shop?
- **How does Tesco add value?** Although this is a question, the word 'how' leads you to provide a description of the ways in which Tesco could add value and therefore limits your chance to show your skills of analysis and evaluation.
  Alternative: Is the Tesco Clubcard the most important way in which Tesco adds value?
- **What motivates workers in company X?** Again, this type of question leads you to give a description of the factors that influence motivation at company X rather than an evaluation of which factors are most important to the firm or to the workers.
  Alternative: Is pay the most important factor in motivating workers at company X?
- **A business plan.** Investigations with such titles are invariably poor. They are often too long and simplistic with insufficient information. Most business plans produced by students conclude that their businesses will be a success. Try to select one aspect of the business plan on which you can base your question.

Alternatives: How reliable is the market research used in my business plan? How important is location to the possible success of my planned business?

- **Why has agriculture/industry/manufacturing/retailing etc. changed in my area?** This question is too broad. The answer is likely to be a list of ways in which the chosen industry has changed, offering no opportunity for evaluation.
Alternative: Is X the main cause of the changes in Y in region Z?

Further suggestions

- To what extent will the proposed ban on smoking affect the three pubs in my village?
- What is the most significant reason for the success of the Pink Ladies taxi business in Warrington?
- What is the main reason for the different interest rates in Japan, the USA and the UK?
- To what extent was the downturn in the economy the reason for the slump in sales of the fashion chain Next over Christmas 2005?
- How serious will the long-term impact be on sales for Scandinavian firm Arla in the Middle East following the cartoon controversy?
- What was the main cause of the difference in the price of flights from London to Paris during February 2006?
- What was the most important reason for the failure to complete the new Wembley Stadium on time?
- To what extent has Vodafone's global expansion strategy been a success?
- What is the main reason for the failure of Golden Wonder to compete in a £2 billion market?
- To what extent has the new supermarket in my town affected small traders?

Note how each of the above questions has been phrased to give the greatest opportunity to address all of the assessment objectives. The questions were inspired by browsing the Biz/ed 'In the News' archive (**www.bized.ac.uk**), which contains short news items relevant to business and economics and could give you some ideas on which you can build your investigations.

Structuring your investigation

In answering any question, you should frame your investigation around the factors related to the knowledge covered in Modules 1, 2 or 3. A topical issue provides you with a context in which you can apply this knowledge. By explaining each of the factors (no more than four are necessary) you can demonstrate your analytical skills. You need also to make some judgements about the relative importance of the factors in your answer. This shows your skills in evaluation and allows you to draw a conclusion.

For example, take the question 'What was the main cause of the difference in the price of flights from London to Paris during February 2006?' The knowledge needed for this question relates to factors that affect markets, which are discussed in all three modules. You may decide that the main causes of difference in price are the level of demand and the level of supply.

You need to find out how much flights cost at different times of the month. You may discover that prices peak around the middle of the month, possibly near 14 February. You have to explain why the prices differ so much. Is it because of the supply of flights? Is it because of the demand for flights and, if so, what causes the change in demand? Your investigation should uncover several factors that could cause the price differences. You could also look at price elasticity of demand for flights at certain times of the month, such as during school holidays. Once you have explained why each factor could give rise to a price difference, you can draw some conclusions about which factor is the most important contributor.

Answers to any of the suggested questions can be constructed in a similar way to give you the best opportunity to meet the assessment objectives. Some investigations require you to carry out primary research, whereas others are more suited to secondary research. The important point is that you address all of the assessment objectives in your answer.

Content Guidance

The first section looks at the content in **Change 1: What are the challenges?** There are five key questions:

- **How do markets change?** This question deals with factors that affect demand and supply and cause changes to income distribution, equity and efficiency.
- **Rivalry or collaboration?** The growth of firms and the strategies used in competition are the focus of this question.
- **Will total output change?** The emphasis in this question switches to the macro-economy with a view on aggregate demand and supply and the causes of economic growth.
- **Unemployment or inflation?** This deals with the relationship between unemployment and inflation and asks whether there is a trade-off between them.
- **Why trade?** Trade offers many benefits but they can be affected by changes in exchange rates, which influence global trade patterns.

The second section looks at the content in **Change 2: Which way forward?** There are five key questions:

- **Why are business plans important?** This question discusses the importance of planning in generating business success.
- **What makes markets grow?** Markets grow because of the dynamics of business — the constant search for new products to capture existing or new markets.
- **What makes an economy grow?** Economies grow because of their productive potential. This question is linked to the quantity and the quality of resources in the economy.
- **Can we control the economy?** Governments adopt fiscal and monetary policies as a means of controlling economic growth.
- **What should governments spend?** Governments impose taxes in order to raise funds to spend on a wide variety of public services.

What are the challenges?

How do markets change?

In the Unit 1 guide in this series, you met the following formula for the main factors that affect demand:

$$D = f (P_n, P_n...P_{n-1}, Y, T, Pop, A, E)$$

This means that the level of demand (D) is dependent upon the factors in brackets:

- P_n — the price of the good.
- $P_n...P_{n-1}$ — the price of substitutes and complements. A substitute is something that can be used instead of the good in question — for example, a pair of Adidas trainers is a substitute for a pair of Nike trainers. A complement is a good that tends to be purchased along with another — a computer needs software to make it useful.
- Y — the level of disposable income.
- T — the tastes and fashions that influence purchasing decisions.
- Pop — the level and structure of the population.
- A — the level of advertising.
- E — the expectations of consumers in making purchasing decisions.

These factors are useful when looking at how markets change. Some of them are changes that occur over time. The reasons for gradual change can sometimes be difficult to identify and to predict.

Mobile phones, internet developments, rises in fuel and energy prices and the ways in which people work and enjoy leisure activities have changed modern life dramatically since the 1990s. As a result, some markets have declined gradually. Businesses have to adapt to these differences and be flexible in their approach to such changing markets. For example, firms such as Vodafone see a future in 3G technology. They have invested huge sums of money for the right to be in the market, but is it turning out to be as lucrative as expected?

Other large firms that were powerful in the mid-1990s, such as Marconi, have experienced major declines in their fortunes. The manufacture of video players is largely disappearing as DVDs take over. The growth of low-cost airlines has changed the way in which people travel and how they enjoy their leisure time.

All of these changes can be linked to the factors that affect demand. Longer-term trends in the economy are known as **structural changes**. When the structure of the economy changes, some businesses disappear but there are opportunities for new ones to take their place. However, the new businesses do not necessarily require the same skills or produce the same products. This influences how the economy as a whole copes with structural changes.

The effects can be seen in the case of the Rover Longbridge plant in the West Midlands. In April 2005, Rover announced that it had gone into administration: 6,000 jobs were lost and the impact on the local area was huge, affecting property prices, incomes, local businesses, Rover's suppliers, dealers across the country etc. After 1 year, only about one-third of the workers had found new jobs, many of which were at lower wages. The site is still redundant and it may be some time before any new business activity is seen at Longbridge.

Income

The amount of money that people have available to spend (**disposable income**) does not depend only on wages earned. The growth of credit and debt and greater access to financial services also contribute to higher income levels. As house prices rise, homeowners can borrow money on the equity in their property — the difference between the increased value of a house and the loan originally taken out to buy it (the mortgage). Borrowed money can be spent on holidays, leisure activities, home improvements, cars etc., so businesses that offer these goods and services benefit in turn from increased income levels.

Tastes

Tastes depend on fashions or social changes. The increased popularity of vegetarianism and a greater emphasis on recycling are examples of social changes that influence demand and alter markets. Higher numbers of women in the workplace, the fashion for more exotic drinks and an increase in demand for different cuisines have each had significant effects on modern life.

Population

The size of a population and its structure can also cause changes in markets. The UK population is undergoing significant change as the number of people aged over 65 rises. This has profound long-term implications for many markets. The Office for National Statistics (ONS) has reported that the UK population has grown by 7% in the last 30 years. The proportion of people aged over 65 has risen from 13% to over 16%. Members of this age group are also living longer. This has an effect on housing provision, benefits, social services, health, education and the types of goods and services demanded, because there is a shift towards satisfying the needs of this older age group.

In addition, there is a smaller proportion of people in the working-age group, which pays taxes to help support the ageing population. In turn, this has a great impact on pension provision. Many businesses have faced real challenges in managing their pension schemes and some types of scheme have been abandoned because they are simply not affordable.

Advertising

Developments in technology have brought about massive changes to modern life, and businesses are keen to ensure that customers know about them. Advertising is an important way of letting consumers know about a business and the goods or services that it offers. The influence of advertising on demand is subtle — why do tobacco companies insist on using Formula 1 as an advertising medium if it does not sell extra cigarettes? Does having the name of a business on the front of a football shirt make a difference to sales? Are clever television adverts just a form of entertainment? Few firms would waste millions of pounds on advertising if it did not bring benefits that were greater than the investment. Advertising does change behaviour — the message gets through gradually.

Expectations

Consumers base their consumption decisions on a number of expectations. For example, when considering whether to buy a flat-screen television, consumers may factor in how secure they feel in their jobs, whether the price of the good is likely to decrease or how they think interest rates may change. In some cases, even the weather can influence whether consumers buy a product. For example, if hot weather is predicted, consumers may be tempted to purchase garden furniture or barbecue equipment.

Many of the factors that influence demand are linked with changes in the political landscape and national debates about how money is raised and spent by government. The aim is to ensure that the public gets what it wants and there are inevitable differences in the best way of achieving this — simply another aspect of resource allocation.

Public and private funding

The growth in public/private initiatives for providing goods and services is discussed in Unit 2. The current Labour government has put forward programmes of radical change in health, education and other public services. It is no longer unusual for a road to be managed by a private company or a bridge to be built by a private/public partnership. Some schools are financed in part by private companies that can make decisions about the direction of the school and how it spends money.

In all these cases it is important to consider the impact on equity and efficiency. Will some schools give their students an unfair advantage? Will public money be spent more efficiently by contracting a private firm to build a new road?

The organisation of the 2012 London Olympic Games illustrates these points. Much of the construction work for the Games will be carried out by private-sector organisations in conjunction with public bodies. The parts of east London that will host the

Games will attract much investment. Inhabitants of these areas may benefit from better housing, transport, social and leisure facilities and open spaces. What about people living in neighbouring boroughs? Will funds be diverted to Stratford at the expense of Barking and Dagenham? Will businesses be tempted to move from other parts of London and the southeast to take advantage of opportunities in the Olympic area? Will it become easier to attract people into public-service work in the southeast — a problem caused partly by a lack of affordable housing — or will the situation worsen?

You should always be aware of the trade-offs that exist in any economic and business decision-making. As markets change, there will be benefits and losses. In exam questions you may be asked to analyse and evaluate how businesses, individuals and government cope with these changes. You can also base your portfolio investigations on similar issues.

Rivalry or collaboration?

Rivalry is an element of competition. A firm must compete against its rivals to capture and retain customers. Methods of competing can be categorised as **price** and **non-price** strategies.

Price strategies

A firm can either cut or raise its prices to capture customers. It would need to justify any price increases.

Penetration pricing

This pricing strategy is used by firms that want to penetrate and increase sales in a market, often when launching a new product. Prices are set much lower than those charged by the rest of the market in order to capture market share quickly. This strategy is associated with high-volume sales and relatively low margins.

Market skimming

Market skimming means that firms charge a relatively high price for a product in order to maximise the benefit of sales over a short period at high margins. This strategy is sometimes used in the clothing industry. The life cycle of the products tends to be short, so when a new season's ranges are launched they often have high prices. Consumers who want to keep up with fashions and buy these products pay a high mark-up. Unsold clothes are then put on sale ahead of the launch of the next season's range.

Many firms have adopted heavy discounting in response to a slowdown in sales. This has had an effect on the way in which consumers shop. They tend to wait for the sales to start because they can get better value for money. This means that market skimming in the clothing industry may be less effective in the future.

Destroyer pricing

The aim of destroyer pricing is to force rivals out of the market. It is particularly effective for larger firms that benefit from economies of scale — they have lower average costs and can afford to cut prices and margins to low levels, which puts pressure on smaller rivals. Smaller firms have higher average costs and if they want to compete, they have to sell their products at a loss, which cannot be sustained over a long period.

Psychological pricing

Psychological pricing aims to give the impression that a good or service is cheaper than it is. Selling a good at £2.99 instead of £3.00 is said to affect consumer behaviour.

Buy one, get one free

The tactic of buy one, get one free (BOGOF) is widespread, especially in supermarkets. Again, economies of scale allow these large organisations to use this strategy. Prices are halved only on selected goods and at certain times, instead of making wholesale price reductions across the entire product range.

Discounting

Discounting is the practice of reducing prices of goods and services. Certain times of the year are associated with heavy discounting, especially if a firm has excess stock to clear. It is better to get some contribution to variable costs through charging reduced prices than to get no revenue at all.

Price fixing

Price fixing is illegal in the UK and Europe. It means either that firms act together to set prices at a level that benefits them, or that an agreement is made to fix prices above the normal market rate. Price fixing is difficult to prove and firms can always offer reasons why a price seems to be higher than market rates.

Price fixing can also be linked to **resale price maintenance**. This occurs when a firm supplies a good to another business on the understanding that its resale price will not be less than a recommended value. In the UK this practice is illegal.

Price wars

Price wars occur if a firm cuts prices in an attempt to gain some advantage, such as capturing market share. Rivals react by reducing their prices, too, and the cycle repeats itself. Price wars have little long-term benefit for the firms in an industry. They tend to occur in markets in which there are few firms or where several large companies dominate the market. Eventually all firms involved in price wars incur smaller margins and may not achieve their desired market share; they may also experience reduced profits.

Non-price strategies

Non-price strategies include all the other ways in which a firm tries to compete with its rivals, such as:

- promotion
- after-sales service
- emphasis on quality
- special offers
- advertising
- reputation
- image
- branding

Branding is a particularly important method of non-price competition. A brand creates an identity that customers associate with a product or service, and does not just mean an exclusive clothing label or fashion house. Having a brand means that consumers recognise your product and are aware of it. A brand reflects the image of the company and can represent what the company wants to be associated with. It is designed to raise the profile of the product with consumers.

Many larger firms manufacture a variety of similar products, but each one is a different brand. Persil is a brand produced by Unilever, which also owns the brands Surf and Lux, as well as Ben and Jerry's, Domestos, Bovril, Timotei and Pot Noodle.

Clothing retailers Poundstretcher, Matalan, Wilkinsons and Primark do not have the same target market as Gucci, Prada and Harrods, but they are all brands. They all cultivate an image and a culture that help their target consumers to understand what they offer. For instance, Primark sells good-quality, functional clothing at reasonable prices and does not see itself in direct competition with companies such as Prada.

Think of any brand and you can make an association — the logo, packaging, ambience, quality, reputation etc. These characteristics form the identity and personality of the brand and make branding an important source of non-price competition. It persuades customers to buy the product again and again. These repeat purchases are an important source of long-term growth for a business.

Business growth

Businesses can grow either *internally* or *externally*.

Internal growth

Internal growth is financed by reinvestment of profits in the business to acquire new equipment, more employees, new buildings, a more efficient plant and so on. This investment allows the firm to increase output and, assuming it can sell what it produces, the business generates further profits, which can also be reinvested.

External growth

External growth results from mergers or takeovers. Mergers occur when two (or more) firms agree to join together. The new firm generally retains some identity from each original company. Examples include Cadbury Schweppes, GlaxoSmithKline and Alliance Boots. A takeover (or acquisition) occurs when one firm buys a controlling interest in another. The firm that is taken over usually loses its identity — for example, the gradual replacement of the Safeway name by Morrisons, as a result of the takeover in 2004.

Mergers and takeovers can also be described as **integrations**, which are either 'vertical' or 'horizontal':

- **Vertical integration** — the merger or takeover of firms at different stages of the production process. If the manufacturer of Levi Strauss jeans decided to buy a chain of retail stores to sell its products exclusively, this would be an example of **vertical integration forwards** (i.e. towards the market). If the integration is towards the source, it is referred to as **vertical integration backwards** — for example, if the jeans manufacturer bought a cotton plantation to secure supplies of raw cotton.
- **Horizontal integration** — the merger or takeover of firms at the same stage of the production process. An example is the attempted takeover of Marks and Spencer by Philip Green, who owns a number of high-street retail stores including Dorothy Perkins, Top Shop, BHS and Miss Selfridge.

The reasons why mergers and takeovers take place include: *fame*

- **Acquisition of a brand name**. Acquisitions allow firms to benefit from the kudos of a brand name without having to invest time and money in building a brand.
- **Rationalisation**. This refers to cases in which businesses can reduce any unnecessary duplication of activities. For example, plants or offices can be closed and resources reallocated to different locations, helping to reduce costs. Overheads such as administration can also be decreased, cutting costs further.
- **Economies of scale**. Acquisitions mean that firms can take advantage of the benefits of economies of scale, which can lead to a reduction in unit costs.
- **Synergies**. Synergy is often explained through the analogy of $2 + 2 = 5$ — the whole is greater than the sum of its parts. These synergies can arise if two firms have particular strengths that complement each other. Merging makes the combined businesses stronger and more competitive.
- **Diversification**. Firms may want to diversify their product or service range in order to get into new markets or to spread their risks. This can help to insulate them from changes in the economic climate.
- **Acquisition of new technology**. Large firms often look for small thriving businesses that have developed new technologies which can be exploited, particularly if the smaller firm has already taken all the investment risks.
- **Market power**. Acquisitions can give firms a greater degree of control over the market.

Acquisition success

In spite of the numerous good reasons for mergers and takeovers, there is no guarantee that the new business will be a success. You need to be aware that not every merger or takeover is successful. Acquiring other businesses presents firms with several challenges:

- The cultures of the businesses may be different or incompatible, which can create friction.
- Morale and motivation can be affected if employees have to be made redundant or relocated.
- Management styles in the two companies may be different and this can lead to friction and inefficiency.
- Bringing processes and systems into line may create a number of problems that can be expensive to solve. For example, Morrisons has experienced difficulties in rebranding its recently acquired Safeway stores. Firms may operate incompatible accounting programs, use different software to do the same job or run different operating systems on their computers.
- The larger firm in an integration can experience diseconomies of scale, especially in communication and decision-making. This can have an adverse effect on its unit costs.

You must be able to balance out the reasons for a merger with the possible difficulties that may face the firms involved. Be selective in your analysis and evaluation of any acquisitions that you have to discuss in exam questions or in your portfolio investigations — not every reason will apply to all mergers or takeovers.

Will total output change?

Addressing this question shifts the focus from microeconomies (individual markets) to the **macroeconomy** — the economy as a whole. The word 'economy' is used widely, but often it is not given any clear definition. Understanding what is meant by 'the economy' is important in putting the elements of this section into context.

The UK economy consists of all the exchange and production activities in the UK.

Similarly, the European economy refers to all the production and exchange activities in the whole of Europe. Every day, millions of decisions are made in buying and selling. Each of these decisions is not that important, but together they have a massive influence on the lives of millions of people, affecting major trends such as economic growth, unemployment, inflation and trade. Macroeconomics looks at these major economic factors. You may not think they have a great effect and they can seem remote, but they do have an impact on our lives in many ways.

The business cycle

Economic activity — the amount of buying and selling that goes on in an economy — tends to follow a cycle. Some periods are characterised by rising levels of economic activity, which can be followed by periods in which economic activity slows down and, in some cases, becomes seriously low.

The tendency of economic activity to follow these cyclical patterns is called the **business cycle** — a crucial concept in understanding change. Note that a period of high economic activity is not followed inevitably by a slump. Equally, a recession is not always the precursor to inflation.

Since the mid-1990s the UK has enjoyed stable economic activity. Inflation and unemployment have been relatively low; economic growth has been healthy but not excessive. Although it could be argued therefore that the cycle no longer exists, this would be incorrect. It may be that the cycle is not as pronounced as in earlier periods when the UK did seem to lunge from 'boom' to 'bust'. However, there have been recent periods when the level of economic growth has slowed down and unemployment has risen. Equally, economic growth has been healthy and there have been concerns about the potential inflationary pressures in the economy.

GDP
GNP

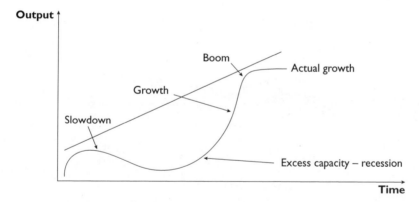

Figure 1 The business cycle

Figure 1 illustrates the main phases of the business cycle. The straight line represents potential growth — the level of growth that would be expected if the economy developed naturally. It is the maximum capacity of the economy to produce goods and services if every available resource is used to its maximum.

However, actual growth is not smooth and predictable — in Figure 1 it is sharp initially and approaches the potential growth curve before decreasing. This fall marks the beginning of a period of **slowdown** in economic activity. If the slowdown persists, the economy could face a **recession**. A recession is defined as **two consecutive quarters of negative economic growth**. In Figure 1 the difference between actual and potential growth is large, suggesting that many resources are not being used — leading to unemployment. When actual growth starts to rise again, it approaches the potential growth curve. If it continues to rise, other problems can follow.

Excessive growth can put pressure on resources — as supplies of raw materials, capital and labour become scarcer, the price of these resources is forced upwards and businesses pass on these increased costs to consumers in the form of higher prices. This is how **inflationary pressure** builds up.

This traditional analysis of the business cycle has been questioned by the 2004 Nobel prizewinners F. E. Kydland and E. C. Prescott. Their research suggests that there may be times when economic growth is slowing but prices actually increase. They prefer to think of the business cycle as a situation in which economic activity deviates from the norm, rather than as an inevitable or evolutionary cyclical process.

Circular flow of income

Economic activity refers to the level of production and exchange in an economy. The circular flow of income explains how the processes of production and exchange are central to the way in which an economy works.

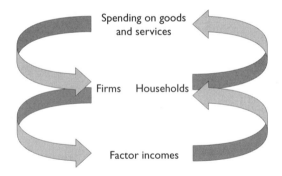

Figure 2 Circular flow of income

Figure 2 is based around two main economic units: firms and households. Households represent all the individuals in an economy, and firms are productive business organisations. Households are the owners of the **factors of production** — land, labour and capital — which they sell to firms in return for **factor incomes** — wages, rent, interest and profit. Firms use the factors of production to offer goods and services, which they sell to households — hence the *circular* flow. This simple model contains the essence of how an economy works and explains the degree of interdependence that exists in any economy.

The explanation above is a simplified version of circular flow. It does not take into account the impact of taxation, savings, imports and exports, but these variables can be built in easily. At this level of study, you need only a basic understanding of the concept of circular flow.

Aggregate demand

Aggregate demand is the sum of all the expenditure in an economy during a period of time. It is summarised in the following formula:

$AD = C + I + G + (X - M)$

- C = **consumption expenditure** — spending on goods and services by members of the public (e.g. clothing, food, leisure, entertainment, household appliances, carpets, furniture).
- I = **investment** — spending by businesses on equipment, machinery and buildings that contribute to production.
- G = **government spending** — accounts for nearly 40% of all spending in the economy (e.g. roads, transport, health, education, defence, justice).
- $(X - M)$ = **net exports** — the amount earned in revenue from selling goods abroad (exports) minus the amount spent on buying goods and services from abroad (imports); $(X - M)$ is referred to as net imports or net exports.

Aggregate demand can be used to calculate **national income** or **gross domestic product**. Gross domestic product (GDP) is a measure of the value of all goods and services produced in an economy during a period of time. In effect, it takes into account the value of every transaction in the economy (in simple terms, value is the quantity of the good or service multiplied by the price).

Aggregate demand is the sum of all expenditures in the economy that occur when one person/group/business/organisation buys a good or service from another. Each transaction involves expenditure by one party and an income for the other. National income and national expenditure measure the same thing and should, in theory, be identical. In reality, however, the complexity of the economy means that national income does not equal national expenditure. Many transactions are not recorded because they are part of the so-called 'black economy', but this does not detract from the basic principle.

A change in any of the components of aggregate demand affects the whole economy and GDP. Aggregate demand is important in economic analysis because a change in GDP is a measure of economic growth.

Consumption

Consumption expenditure is affected by income levels, wealth, tax levels, availability of credit, expectations about work, product marketing and so on. For example, a recent report suggests that wealth will rise in future years as a result of the increased value of houses, which will eventually be passed on through inheritance.

Investment

The level of investment depends on the prevailing economic conditions — particularly the expectations of producers and advances in technology. If producers think that demand will be buoyant in coming months or years, they are more likely to invest in expanding capacity. The interest rate or expected return from the investment could influence decisions to invest.

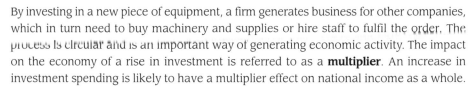

By investing in a new piece of equipment, a firm generates business for other companies, which in turn need to buy machinery and supplies or hire staff to fulfil the order. The process is circular and is an important way of generating economic activity. The impact on the economy of a rise in investment is referred to as a **multiplier**. An increase in investment spending is likely to have a multiplier effect on national income as a whole.

Government

The government has a major influence on the level of economic activity, since its spending accounts for nearly 40% of GDP. Government tax and spending decisions are watched closely by analysts because they can have a significant impact on the economy. Signs that the government will have to raise tax rates to support its spending plans may be greeted with some concern by the City because of the effect this can have on consumption and therefore on aggregate demand and GDP.

Exports and imports

In simple terms, exports may be regarded as beneficial. If foreign countries want to buy UK goods and services, it shows that the products are competitive and good quality. An export involves the purchase of a good or service from a UK-based business that causes a flow of income into the country — i.e. a credit on the UK trading account. In contrast, imports are purchases of goods and services from abroad that take money out of the country — a debit on the UK trading account. Imports in themselves are not harmful, but there must be a balance between levels of imports and exports. If imports are greater than exports (as is usually the case in the UK), this has a negative impact on overall aggregate demand.

Aggregate supply

The other side of the macroeconomic equation is aggregate supply — a measure of the ability of the country to produce goods and services, which gives an indication of the capacity of the economy. At any price level, producers are willing to supply a certain amount, which depends on the resources available and their judgement on the expected return from production.

Aggregate supply is affected by:
- expectations of producers
- price of inputs (land, labour and capital)
- productivity levels
- flexibility of the labour market (the ease with which labour can be reallocated to different uses)
- level of technology
- quality of capital (e.g. how productive machinery is)
- availability of natural resources

Aggregate demand and supply analysis

As with market demand and supply in microeconomics, the aggregate demand and supply model can be used to analyse changes in the macroeconomy. The model can be represented as a graph with price level on the vertical axis (changes in which can be linked to the effect on inflation) and national income on the horizontal axis. Any change in national income reflects variations in economic growth. The model yields useful information about the workings of the macroeconomy and the trade-offs that may need to be made between growth and price level.

In Figure 3, aggregate demand is shown as a downward-sloping curve from left to right, representing its relationship with the price level in an economy. In theory, a fall in the price level could be caused by or affect interest rates or the exchange rate and also lead to an increase in personal wealth.

A lower price level is associated with reduced interest rates, a lower exchange rate and a rise in personal wealth, because the value of money is greater. All these conditions encourage consumers and businesses to spend more. Hence, a lower price level is associated with a greater level of national income. Aggregate supply is represented as an upward-sloping curve from left to right. This shows that at higher price levels suppliers are willing to offer more goods for sale.

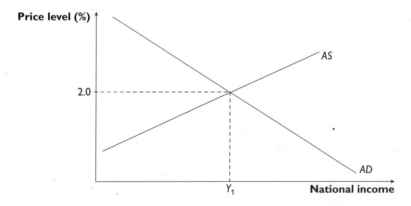

Figure 3 Aggregate demand and supply curves

Where the *AD* and *AS* curves intersect is a point of **equilibrium** in the economy. Remember that this is only a model that helps in analysing the possible outcomes of changes in an economy. It is unlikely that an economy ever reaches equilibrium. In Figure 3 the level of national income is shown as Y_1 with the price level (inflation) at 2%.

The equilibrium point is a good starting position for analysing what can happen following changes in either aggregate demand or supply. For example, what does the model predict will happen if government increases income tax rates on those earning higher incomes from 40% to 45%?

Tax rates on high earners affect aggregate demand and the income levels of this group would be likely to decrease. Depending on the proportion of high earners in the working population, this could affect consumption expenditure. A further complication would arise if the government decided to increase spending as its tax revenue rose. The overall effect on aggregate demand depends on the difference between the effects on consumption expenditure and government spending.

Assuming that the impact on consumption is greater than the effect on government spending, the *AD* curve shifts to the left as consumption falls (Figure 4). At every price level, less is spent than before the tax change.

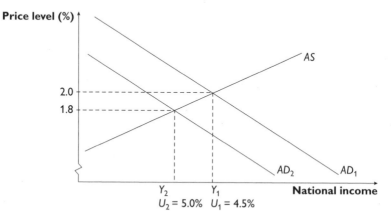

Figure 4 Effect of a fall in **AD**

The overall effect on the economy is a reduction in price level from 2.0% to 1.8% and in national income from Y_1 to Y_2. The fall in national income can be linked directly to the level of unemployment. A certain level of output requires a specific level of labour to produce it (other factors being equal). If output levels fall, less labour is needed. Therefore, a fall in national income is associated with a possible rise in unemployment. In Figure 4 the level of unemployment at the first equilibrium position is U_1 (4.5%) and U_2 (5.0%) at the new equilibrium position. The value $(U_2 - U_1)$ represents the rise in unemployment.

This analysis points out the trade-offs that have to be considered in economic policy-making. The government's decision may have caused a slowdown in the rate of growth of prices (inflation), which, though desirable, is at the expense of a rise in unemployment. Is a rise in unemployment an acceptable price to pay to slow down inflation?

Aggregate demand and supply analysis is a useful tool for looking at changes in the economy. You must always bear in mind, however, that this is just a model — it is difficult to integrate the complexities of the economy fully in such a model, so your conclusions must be made with caution.

The Treasury uses a similar model of the economy to assess the likely impact of changes in economic variables. The Institute of Fiscal Studies, the ITEM Club and other City financial analysts also employ models of the economy that are based on aggregate supply and demand. These are complex econometric models that permit changes in many variables at once. At AS, the model serves simply to introduce you to the tools that economists use to analyse and assess macroeconomic changes, and examiners

content guidance

expect you to make some elementary use of these models in your analysis. The Question and Answer section helps you to see how models can be applied in analysis.

Unemployment or inflation?

The trade-off between growth and the price level has already been discussed. Questions are now being raised about the extent of this trade-off, particularly by the Nobel prizewinning economists, Kydland and Prescott. However, in this AS course you should assume that lower levels of national income are associated with higher levels of unemployment and lower price levels (inflation).

The Phillips curve

A. W. Phillips was an economist from New Zealand who investigated the links between price level and unemployment for the period from 1861 to 1957. He found that there was an inverse correlation between the rate of growth of wages and unemployment, which can be expressed as a relationship between inflation and unemployment, known as the **Phillips curve** (Figure 5). Phillips concluded that the trade-off of attempts to reduce unemployment (assuming unemployment is an 'economic evil') is an increase in inflation.

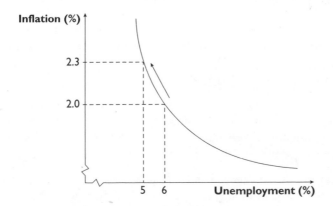

Figure 5 The Phillips curve

If government believes that an unemployment rate of 6% (Figure 5) is unacceptable, it can introduce policies designed to reduce unemployment, which involves boosting the level of output in the economy. This produces a rise in consumption, so suppliers try to increase output to meet the new demand. This puts pressure on resources and the price of factors of production increases as a result. Any increase in factor prices affects aggregate supply and producers may pass on these higher prices to consumers. The net result is an increase in inflation from 2.0% to 2.3% in Figure 5 — this is the trade-off for reducing unemployment from 6% to 5%.

The Phillips curve and our model of aggregate supply and demand are closely linked. Figure 6 shows how a rise in aggregate demand as a result of government action to boost demand (such as reducing tax rates) affects the price level and output and how the Phillips curve can be used to explain this process.

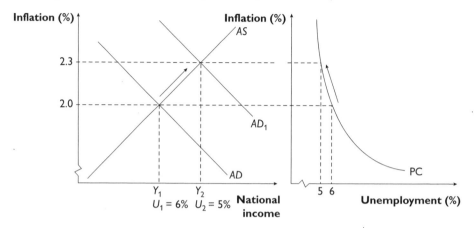

Figure 6 Linking AS/AD and the Phillips curve

The simple trade-off suggested in the Phillips curve has been criticised as the economy has developed. For example, in the 1970s the UK experienced periods of high inflation and rising unemployment levels. This was explained in terms of a shift of the Phillips curve, as a result of the expectations of both producers and consumers about potential changes in the economy. Expectations act as a factor in both aggregate demand and supply. In recent years it has become important to build this variable into models of economic behaviour.

Why is inflation a problem?

Every economy needs some inflation in order to provide incentives for a dynamic economy to operate. For example, since the year 2000, Japan has experienced **deflation** — falling price levels. This has been accompanied by negative economic growth, decreasing wage levels and investment and a serious slump in the economy.

However, high levels of inflation can have equally damaging consequences, including:

- **Effect on the value of money**. High levels of inflation affect the value of money. If rates of pay do not keep up with inflation rates, real incomes fall and consumers are unable to buy as many goods and services with their income as before.
- **Effect on investment**. In times of rising prices, firms are reluctant to invest because of the uncertainty in the economy. Investment decisions are based on the cost of the investment and the expected returns — often over a number of years. In times when prices are rising, this return is harder to calculate. If prices rise by 4% one year, 6% the following year and 5% the year after, it becomes difficult for businesses to plan ahead.
- **Menu costs**. In times of inflation, businesses need to adjust the prices of their goods and services. Therefore, they incur additional costs because systems have to be updated or price labels changed.

- **Effect on savings**. Inflation rates affect savings levels. Savings accounts may be tied to an interest rate that is less than the rate of inflation. This could reduce the standard of living of people who rely on savings for income.
- **Influence on people with fixed incomes**. People living on fixed incomes that do not rise with inflation also experience a drop in their standard of living.
- **Distortions to financial markets**. Companies that lend money in times of high inflation will be worse off when the loan is repaid, unless the interest rate changes in line with inflation. This is because the money repaid after several years will not buy as much as when the loan was made. In contrast, the borrower benefits because the value of the money to be repaid at the end of the loan period is less than that when borrowed. Such distortions affect the distribution of wealth in the economy as well as the incentives for those involved.

The short and long term

When using aggregate demand and supply analysis it is important to distinguish between the short term and the long term. The **short term** is the period of time within which some factors of production cannot be changed. The **long term** is the period of time in which all factors of production can be altered. This distinction allows some understanding of how businesses may react to changing economic conditions to be built into the analysis. For example, suppose that the government announces a significant rise in spending. This causes the *AD* curve to shift to the right and increases national income. This rise in national income assumes that firms can respond to the changes in the economy by expanding output — taking on labour and securing the resources needed to increase output.

In the short run, there may be a number of supply constraints that prevent this expansion. In the long run, the *AS* curve may be vertical — there is a notional maximum capacity that the economy is capable of producing, which assumes that all factors of production are employed at maximum capacity and efficiency. If government seeks to boost demand at times when the economy is at or close to maximum capacity, the effect of the measure is markedly different from that when the economy is operating well below maximum capacity.

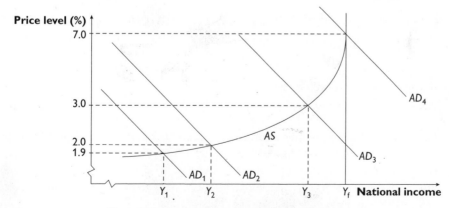

Figure 7 *Long-run aggregate supply curve*

In Figure 7, the AS curve gets gradually steeper as it approaches the long-run, full-employment output — Y_f (maximum capacity). If the initial equilibrium position is found at the intersection of the AS curve with AD_1, the economy is operating well below Y_f. An increase in demand to AD_2 is accompanied by an increase in national income (from Y_1 to Y_2) and a minimal rise in price level (from 1.9 to 2.0). This is because businesses have the capacity to expand and use previously redundant resources relatively easily.

Compare this with a situation in which the initial equilibrium is given by the intersection of AS with AD_3. In this case, the spare capacity in the economy is limited. Any boost in demand at this level puts a strain on the economy's resources. Firms attempting to expand output would encounter difficulties in getting resources because they would be in short supply. This is known as a 'bottle neck'. As a result, the increase in national income is only small but the trade-off is a relatively large rise in the price level (from 3% to 7%).

When analysing the impact of changes in the economy, you should bear in mind the existing conditions. In reality, many economic indicators are subtle. A current growth rate of 3% may be considered too high to sustain any growth in demand without causing inflationary pressures, but a growth rate of 2.8% may be thought perfectly healthy.

Textbooks tend to show large differences between growth and inflation rates in order to highlight the effect. However, you need to be aware of the levels of the key economic indicators and how they are changing in order to make sense of the analysis in your answers. You can do this by keeping abreast of the main changes in the economy. The Office for National Statistics (ONS) (**www.ons.gov.uk**) produces monthly figures on unemployment, growth and inflation. In general, they are easy to understand and not too long. You should take a regular look at what is happening to improve your understanding and awareness.

Why trade?

Most countries engage in trade. At the simplest level, a country trades when it has a surplus of products that it can exchange for goods or services that it cannot produce (or produce as efficiently as the other country). International trade brings a range of benefits, including:

- **Acquiring goods that cannot be produced**. Some countries do not have the resources or the climate to produce certain goods, which can be acquired instead through international trade.
- **Efficiencies from specialisation and exchange**. International trade leads to efficient allocation of resources. Some countries have access to skills and resources that allow them to produce goods and services more efficiently and at lower cost than elsewhere. The efficiency gains from trade can also lead to lower world prices and the benefits of economies of scale.

- **Economic growth**. International trade gives greater potential for economic growth in a country, which affects employment and raises the standard of living.

The trade in goods and services is referred to as 'imports and exports'. It is important to remember that imports and exports are linked to the movements of funds across the world. It is equally crucial to bear in mind that international trade is the result of millions of decisions taken by individuals throughout the world on how they spend their money. Governments may monitor trade flows through the balance of payments, but they do not *control* international trade.

The level of imports and exports is a useful indicator of the competitiveness of an economy in relation to other nations. If exports are rising, it suggests that the quality, price and efficiency of businesses involved in exports are favourable in comparison to those in other countries. Rising import levels may indicate that a country's ability to produce goods and services is not as great as that of its competitors abroad. It could also mean that strong consumer demand is not being met by domestic production, so imports are needed. Increased import levels can occur if resources and equipment are being purchased to contribute to production — a high level of imports is not necessarily undesirable.

The balance of payments

The government records in the balance of payments details of the international transactions that the UK makes. The balance of payments records all the receipts (inflows of funds) that the UK gets from selling goods and services abroad (export earnings) and all the expenditure (outflow of funds) by the UK in buying goods and services from abroad. It is presented as an accounting document. If the spending on imports is greater than the receipts from exports, the balance of payments is said to be in **deficit**. If export receipts exceed spending on imports, there is said to be a **trade surplus**.

The latest data on UK trade show that in the third quarter of 2005 there was a deficit of £2 billion. There are further concepts and terminology associated with the balance of payments that you should investigate further, since this guide outlines only the essential content needed. At this level, however, it is important to understand that such a deficit has to be financed in the same way as if you had a personal income and expenditure account. If you have a deficit on your transactions, you need to find the money to make your account balance. The government has to do the same, because large and persistent deficits in trade have a negative influence on the level of aggregate demand.

Exchange rates

The exchange rate is the price of one currency expressed in terms of another. Exchange rates play a pivotal role in international trade. A UK firm that purchases goods from a US supplier needs to buy US dollars to complete the transaction.

Movements in exchange rates can influence the amount of money that has to be given up to acquire the equivalent amount of foreign currency and so they appear to affect prices. Exchange rates alter because of changes in the supply and demand of currencies on foreign exchange markets. Every day billions of pounds are traded on these exchanges — businesses and individuals buying and selling pounds sterling to acquire the currencies they need to finance transactions. Foreign exchange markets are also influenced by speculation — when traders buy and sell currencies at various prices to make money out of the difference.

Transactions between UK businesses and the USA can be used to examine the effect of exchange rates on trade. Importing goods from the USA to the UK means that sterling must be sold and dollars bought (increasing the supply of pounds on the foreign exchange markets). An increase in the supply of sterling causes a downward pressure on the exchange rate. Exporting goods from the USA to the UK involves selling dollars and buying sterling. Exports create a demand for sterling and put an upward pressure on the exchange rate. In this case, a rise in the sterling exchange rate against the dollar is called an **appreciation** of the exchange rate. This means that the pound is worth more in terms of dollars — for example, a rise in the exchange rate from £1 = $1.67 to £1 = $1.70.

When the pound appreciates, import prices *appear* to fall, while export prices *appear* to rise. This is because a US buyer has to give up more dollars to acquire the same amount of pounds sterling — this gives the impression that export prices are rising. Importers have to give up fewer pounds to acquire the same amount of dollars and so import prices appear to be cheaper.

A fall in the sterling exchange rate against the dollar is called a **depreciation** in the exchange rate. This means that the pound is worth less in terms of dollars — for example, a fall in the exchange rate from £1 = $1.80 to £1 = $1.76. When the pound depreciates, import prices *appear* to rise and export prices *appear* to fall.

A useful way to help remember the effects of exchange rates on import and export prices is the acronym SPICED:
- **s**trong
- **p**ound
- **i**mports
- **c**heaper
- **e**xports
- **d**earer

Thus, movements in exchange rates can affect trade decisions. If the exchange rate is relatively high, UK exporters face difficulties in selling their goods abroad. They have to work hard to convince foreign companies to buy their goods — for example, by cutting their costs, improving efficiency, productivity, quality and after-sales service — in order to make themselves more competitive and to counteract the effect of the exchange rate. However, importers face apparently lower import prices. This can cause demand to be transferred from domestic suppliers to those abroad, which can harm the economy.

The reverse situation may benefit exporters but could lead to an increase in inflationary pressure because import prices are higher. In a country like the UK this is especially relevant because a large proportion of raw materials and semi-finished products are bought in, which increases input costs.

When assessing the effects of exchange rates, it is important to recognise that the overall outcome depends on many factors, including the extent of the change in price, the price elasticity of demand for imports and exports, the quality of the relationships and brand loyalty. Think about the example of a firm that buys in imported raw materials from abroad, manufactures products and sells them to a different overseas market — the complexity of the exchange-rate movements is evident and would need careful consideration.

European monetary union

As a member of the European Union (EU) the UK has been involved in the process of economic and monetary union (EMU) — establishing a single market in the EU and introducing a single currency. The UK has not yet joined the euro but plays a full part in the development of the single market.

Creating a single market involves putting in place systems and laws to facilitate the free movement of goods and services throughout the EU. The introduction of a single currency is intended to make transactions between European states more transparent. The recent expansion of the EU membership and the proposed admission of new members mean that more work is needed to bring about the single market.

Which way forward?

Why are business plans important?

Whether setting up a new business, launching a new product or making an acquisition, planning is vital to success — thinking ahead and taking into account all possibilities mean that a business is better prepared for any eventuality.

Business planning

A new business would be expected to have a business plan that included the following elements:

- **Market research** — some basic market research outlining details of the expected market (e.g. market size and make-up).
- **Competition** — which firms provide competition and how serious is the threat to the prospective business's chances?

- **Competitive advantage** — identify its competitive advantage over rivals — what will make customers buy from the business rather than from anyone else?
- **Financial information** — a detailed cash-flow forecast would be a prerequisite of a business plan, possibly also including a budget outlining proposed income and expenditure for at least the first year.
- **Marketing** — how will the business be promoted? Where and how will it be sold? What will the pricing strategy be?
- **Resources** — an outline of the resources needed, such as a staff profile and details of the location and premises.

Cash flow

Cash flow is an important concept in business planning. One of the main reasons why many new and existing businesses fail is difficulties with cash flow.

Cash flow should not be confused with profit — it is the flow of money into and out of the business. Inflows occur when firms receive revenue from selling goods and services, whereas outflows occur when firms buy raw materials and other inputs — including labour — to carry out production.

Revenue and sales do not always occur at the same time, so it is important to balance the cash coming in and going out. If a firm has debts but no cash to pay them, it can become insolvent (unable to pay its debts) and be forced out of business.

Securing finance

Finance is needed to start up a business. Start-up costs represent most of the fixed costs of a business and include:
- cost of finding premises
- arranging the insurances needed to run a business
- buying stock, fixtures and fittings, equipment or machinery

All of these costs are incurred before any revenue can be generated through sales. Below is a list of the main sources of finance. It is important to remember that not all these sources are available to everyone who starts up a business — for example, a sole trader establishing a painting and decorating business will not be issuing shares on the stock exchange.
- **Bank loans** — many businesses raise finance through a bank loan. Small and medium-sized companies may apply for loans to high-street banks, which usually have dedicated business finance sections. Large businesses are more likely to work with merchant banks that specialise in raising finance for more expensive projects or deals.
- **Savings** — small businesses are often started using savings or money from redundancy payments.
- **Government grants** — the Department for Trade and Industry (DTI) makes available sums of money for businesses in the form of grants. Certain conditions usually have to be fulfilled to get a grant, such as locating the business in a particular area or taking on a set number of employees.

- **Share issues** — private and public limited companies can raise finance by issuing shares in the business. In private limited companies, this requires the agreement of existing shareholders, who may also be asked to subscribe more capital. In the case of public limited companies (plcs), issuing shares can help to finance expansion.
- **Retained profit** — retained profit is only available as a source of finance to businesses that are already trading. Firms set aside a portion of the profit to finance further expansion and investment in the business.

What makes markets grow?

Markets grow because businesses recognise consumer demand and try to offer products and services that meet this demand. It could be argued that there is no need to produce anything new since almost every need is already catered for. However, this would cause markets to stagnate eventually — innovation drives markets.

Innovation

Innovation can take different forms but is usually centred on product development and research and development (R&D). Product development includes:

- **Creating new products** that drive consumer demand. A good example is the replacement of vinyl LPs by cassette tape and then CDs. Similarly, video cassettes have now been superseded by DVDs.
- **Improving existing products** to provide new features or incorporate new technologies, as illustrated by the various generations of the Sony PlayStation.
- **Product extension** — using existing products as the basis for generating new markets — for example, repackaging fruit juices into smaller cartons to satisfy the snack or packed-lunch market. The confectionery company Mars has used its existing products to penetrate other markets (e.g. ice creams and drinks).

Innovation and product development are vital to maintaining or generating competitive advantage. The process by which a product develops and grows can be thought of as a product life cycle. In general, all products go through this process, but the time period may be lengthy for some products and quite short for others. For example, KitKat was first launched in the early 1900s and is still a strong brand today — it therefore has a long life cycle.

Product life cycle

The product life cycle represents the process of change that products go through during their lifetime (Figure 8). It starts with the research and development (R&D) phase, which can last many years or only a few months or weeks. During this period, a firm spends money on developing and testing products that are not generating any revenue. The R&D phase is therefore a drain on resources and finance.

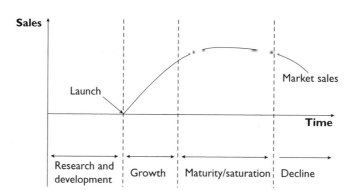

Figure 8 Product life cycle

The next stage in the life cycle is product launch, after which sales begin to grow. Sometimes the growth in sales can be slow as a product becomes established in the market. During the growth phase a business may have to spend money on advertising and promoting the product.

Eventually sales growth begins to slow down and reaches a more stable level. This phase in the life cycle is called maturity. At this point, the business can expect revenues to be generated at little cost, since the product may need only minimal support and promotion. The maturity stage can last for many years for some products, but in the end the product will begin to decline and sales start to fall. During the decline phase, a firm must consider whether to continue to support the product or withdraw it from the market.

Some textbooks include a saturation stage after maturity — when the market is flooded with products of a similar type, causing sales to fall.

A product life cycle is a useful way for a firm to monitor its portfolio. Most large businesses have several products whose life cycles may overlap. This means that established products generate the revenue needed to finance the R&D into new products or to support new launches.

How can sales be increased?

Finding ways to increase sales involves looking at the various marketing strategies based on the four Ps:
- price
- product
- promotion
- place

Some books refer to seven Ps — the four Ps plus packaging, people and process. Whatever the number of components in the marketing mix, businesses need to think about how to link them together in order to target their markets.

It may be that a small price adjustment is needed to boost sales. The product itself could also be altered in order to increase sales. Changing where products are sold (place) may mean moving away from traditional high-street markets and going online or relocating business operations to a new site. For example, Asda and Tesco have each set up CD mail-order services in Jersey. The island has a different government and tax structure to the rest of the UK, which means that the companies can sell chart CDs at much lower prices because they are not subject to VAT in Jersey.

Promotion is another way in which a firm can increase sales. It is not just about advertising but includes the whole range of special offers, vouchers, in-store promotions, user trials and testing and public relations.

When discussing the marketing mix, remember the key word — mix. Few firms focus on just one aspect in their marketing strategy, but some components are more important than others. If the product is a piece of capital equipment, there may be greater focus on the product than on the price, place or promotion. However, this does not mean that the other elements of the marketing mix are not important.

What makes an economy grow?

Growth

Economic growth can be viewed from four different perspectives:
- **Potential growth** — the amount that the economy could produce if it used all its resources to the maximum level.
- **Actual growth** — the recorded level of output in a given time period; this is invariably less than potential growth because some resources are always unemployed.
- **Nominal growth** — the money value of output not counting the impact of any price increases. If GDP rises from £600 billion to £650 billion, how much of this 'growth' is due simply to the increase in prices in the economy?
- **Real growth** — the change in the value of output when changes in prices have been stripped out. Growth from £600 billion to £650 billion in the example above would be due simply to a rise in the volume of output as well as its value.

There are six main factors that can lead to economic growth:
(1) **Quantity and quality of resources**. This includes the quantity and quality of land, labour and capital in the economy. Land that is arid or prone to flooding is less productive than land in areas where the climate is less extreme. Similarly, the quality of capital helps to determine its efficiency and productivity and, together with labour, education and training, it can improve the quality of human capital.
(2) **Infrastructure**. The quality of the infrastructure (e.g. transport links, communication networks, bridges, airports, seaports) can boost the potential output capability in a country.

(3) **Tax and benefits systems**. Government tax and benefits systems are important in developing incentives for businesses and entrepreneurs. New enterprises contribute to future economic growth, so an inflexible tax system will cause the economy to stagnate.

(4) **Regulatory frameworks**. If regulation by the authorities is extensive, the incentive to be creative and to innovate or take risks is reduced. The bureaucracy involved in such situations is called 'red tape'.

(5) **Savings**. The circular flow of income illustrates the degree of interdependence between firms and households (Figure 2). A more sophisticated model of circular flow includes leakages and injections. Not all of a household's income is spent on consumption — some of it is saved. These savings can be invested in banks, pension funds, insurance and assurance policies, shares and so on. In this way, the supply of funds from savings can be used to invest in business and so the level of savings is a contributory factor in economic growth.

(6) **Technology**. This has a direct effect on productivity and production levels. The more sophisticated and readily available the technology, the more productive the economy is.

The role of trade

The Fairtrade movement, the G8 Summit and world trade talks have focused attention on the importance of trade in generating economic growth through wealth creation. Countries use their resources to produce goods and services. Any surplus can be traded with other nations and thus generate wealth that can be reinvested into the country, contributing further to the cycle. Organisations such as the European Union highlight the benefits of opening up borders to trade. Many member states have enjoyed improvements in their trade and economic position as a result of being in the EU.

Removing the restrictions on international trade has been cited as one of the key measures that could reduce poverty and inequality in the world's poorest nations. Richer countries might also benefit from selling their goods in these potentially huge markets. It is difficult to break down existing international trade barriers (subsidies and tariffs) set up by blocs such as the EU and the North American Free Trade Association (NAFTA). Although withdrawing agriculture subsidies would certainly help farmers in less developed countries, many farmers in developed countries would go out of business — a scenario that governments want to avoid.

Can we control the economy?

Governments seek to influence the working of the economy by adopting a range of financial policies.

Fiscal policy

Fiscal policy is concerned with government income and expenditure. The government receives income from taxation and borrowing and spends money on public services such as health, education, social security, transport, defence and law and order. Fiscal policies can be used to influence the level of economic activity.

Tight fiscal policy

If the level of economic activity is too high, the tax system can be adjusted to reduce spending — to slow down the economy. Equally, the government can find ways of cutting back its own expenditure to influence aggregate demand. However, many governments of all political persuasions have found this to be difficult to put into practice.

Loose fiscal policy

In times of economic slowdown the government can relax the tax system and invest more money in the economy through its own spending plans. The aim is to kick-start the process of economic growth. In this way government can have an impact on the following major target areas of policy:

- controlling inflation
- maintaining full employment
- generating sustainable economic growth
- monitoring the exchange rate and the trade balance

These are referred to as **economic policy objectives**. However, fiscal policy is also used to target **non-economic policy objectives**, such as improving the health of the nation or the quality of housing and reducing child poverty. Fiscal policy is therefore bound up with many initiatives and objectives. From the end of the Second World War until the mid-1970s, fiscal policy was the main economic approach in the UK. Since that time it has tended to be used more in support of other policy instruments.

Monetary policy

Monetary policy is the attempt to control the level of economic activity by influencing the price and supply of money — that is, manipulating the interest rate. In 1997, the government gave operational control of monetary policy to the Bank of England with a remit to keep inflation under control. An initial target of 2.5% was set but this has since been reduced to its current target level of 2.0%.

Each month, the Bank of England's Monetary Policy Committee (MPC) meets to discuss the economy and the outlook for inflation. It makes decisions about the bank's lending rate, which influences the structure of interest rates throughout the economy. If the MPC believes that inflationary pressures are rising, it increases interest rates to reduce aggregate demand. If the economy is slowing down, interest rates are reduced. If inflation is outside the target range prescribed by the government, the Bank of England is accountable to the chancellor of the exchequer.

Since the Bank of England took over this responsibility, the UK has experienced a period of stability with historically low interest rates. Its actions have been measured and cautious. Rates have risen or fallen by small amounts — a quarter point at a time — sending a signal to the economy about the bank's intentions and its view on how the economy is performing.

Supply-side policies

Supply-side policies are associated with measures for increasing the long-term capacity of the economy — that is, to shift the aggregate supply curve to the right (see Figure 7). These policies are focused on ways of improving the signals sent to markets to enable them to function more efficiently in allocating scarce resources to competing uses. Key features of such policies include:

- **Education and training** — to improve the quality and flexibility of human capital.
- **Incentives** — adjusting the tax and benefits systems to encourage people to work and make it easier for enterprise to flourish.
- **Improving the efficiency of labour markets** — making it easier for businesses to employ the necessary staff, find the right skills and improve the geographical and occupational mobility of the labour market, thus reducing the rigidities in the labour market that impose additional costs on businesses.
- **Deregulation** — removing regulations on businesses to act in certain ways and cutting back 'red tape'.
- **Privatisation** — finding ways of getting the private sector involved in the provision of public services; the principle is that the private sector has an incentive to provide more efficient services at lower cost.
- **Trade-union reform** — the trade-union movement of the twenty-first century is different from that which existed during the 1960s, 1970s and 1980s; reform has made unions more accountable and the labour market less rigid (an inflexible labour market was believed to underlie problems of low productivity and high costs experienced by businesses).

Exchange-rate policies

Since the collapse of the original exchange-rate mechanism in Europe in the early 1990s, few Western governments have adopted an exchange-rate policy — apart from monitoring the value of currency. However, China has operated a number of controls on its exchange rate. In theory, an exchange-rate policy is used to impose discipline on businesses and the economy. If the government will not allow the exchange rate to be devalued, businesses know that they cannot rely on a depreciation of the exchange rate to make them more competitive. Instead, they have to adopt policies to improve their competitiveness, productivity and efficiency. Increased efficiency helps to keep inflation in check, since domestic producers are not tempted to put up prices when faced with competition from abroad in the hope that the exchange rate will relieve them of their responsibilities — for example, in monitoring costs and increasing productivity.

What should governments spend?

Public expenditure

The government has both economic and non-economic objectives. As in any economic problem, the government is unable to meet all its objectives at once — there have to be trade-offs between the constraints on government spending and the competing demands made on the government. If the government focuses on reducing child poverty, it must divert resources to help those families most in need. Prioritising this policy objective means that other objectives may have to be compromised.

In 2005/06, there have been several high-profile cases concerning the breast-cancer drug Herceptin. The cost to the NHS of providing a course of this treatment is around £20,000 per year per patient. Some health trusts argue that forcing them to offer this drug may mean that patients needing different care have to wait or are refused treatment.

The trade-offs for government are often stark and in many cases have significant effects. Decisions to widen roads or construct bypasses affect communities in different ways. Although the number of accidents may be reduced, there is a great impact on the environment. There is rarely, if ever, a right answer to the question of what the government should spend its money on.

Taxation and borrowing

The government raises money from tax revenue and from borrowing. It borrows by issuing bonds and bills such as Treasury bills and gilt-edged stock or through premium bonds and National Savings schemes. However, most of the government's funds come from taxation. The Unit 1 guide in this series contains a breakdown of the types of tax revenue and what this money is spent on. This section looks at some of the theory behind taxes.

Taxes do not just raise revenue — they are also used to change behaviour and can control consumption. For example, the high taxes on tobacco may act as a disincentive to smokers. In turn, this could release funds in the health service to treat illnesses other than those brought on by smoking. Taxes on leaded petrol were increased at a faster rate than those on unleaded in order to persuade consumers to switch to unleaded fuel cars.

Governments can levy two types of tax:
- **Direct taxes** are placed on incomes, and the individual is ultimately responsible for the payment of the tax.
- **Indirect taxes** are levied on expenditure. The responsibility for paying the tax may lie with shopkeepers, for example, but they can pass on the burden of the tax (who actually pays it in the end) to the customer in the form of higher prices.

Taxes can be imposed in three ways:
- **Progressive taxes** — the rich pay more than the poor; the rate of tax increases as income rises.
- **Proportional taxes** — the rich pay the same proportion of their income in tax as do the poor; the rate of tax is the same at all levels of income.
- **Regressive taxes** — the poor pay a greater amount of tax than the rich. For example, person A earns £1,000 per week and person B earns £100 per week. Both buy a bottle of scotch for £15, £5 of which is tax duty. Both pay the same amount of tax, but the proportion of tax paid by person B is greater than that paid by person A (0.5% for person A and 5% for person B).

The income tax system in the UK is a progressive tax system that operates as follows:
- There is a tax-free allowance on incomes up to £4,895 (2005/06 value).
- A starting tax rate of 10% is levied on incomes ranging from £0 to £2,090 (not including the tax-free allowance).
- The basic rate of tax of 22% is imposed on incomes between £2,091 and £32,400.
- A higher tax rate of 40% is levied on incomes above £32,400.

Redistribution of income

The tax and benefits systems can be used to redistribute income from the rich to the poor. It is not simply a case of taxing the wealthy at a higher rate and giving benefits (e.g. disability allowances, income support, rent rebates, council tax allowances) to those on lower incomes. The basic principle is that the state should provide support for those least able to help themselves. People who are more fortunate have a moral duty to make a contribution — through the tax system — to those who are less fortunate.

However, some people argue that those who have worked hard to build their careers and earn a good income deserve to keep the fruits of their labour and should not have to subsidise those who do not take the opportunities that society offers. This view may be justified if people abuse the benefits system, but it does not address the issue of those who genuinely need the help of the state.

Successive governments have tried to reform the welfare state — the whole benefits system — but this is a highly controversial, complex and expensive task. The attempts often result in minor adjustments to benefits but no wholesale reform of the tax and benefits system.

Questions
&
Answers

This section includes an example of one question from each section of the Unit 2 paper. The style of the questions is similar to that used in the actual exam paper.

Examples of typical candidate responses are provided, together with examiner's comments preceded by the icon 🄔.

You can work through this section in different ways:
- Use the questions as a practice exam that you attempt during your revision.
- Check your answers against the responses provided and assess your performance.
- Study the candidates' answers in detail — try to pick out their good and bad points.
- Use the examiner's comments to help you avoid making mistakes and to maximise your chances of writing what the examiner wants to read.

However you choose to use this section, remember that an important part of your revision involves putting into practice the knowledge and the skills that you have developed. It is strongly recommended that you tackle as many practice questions as you can in the run-up to the exam.

Ensure that you keep in mind the assessment objectives. Note the command words used in the question, which, together with the number of marks available, give you a good guide to how much detail is required and which assessment objectives are being targeted.

Remember that the content examined in Unit 2 is drawn from both Module 2 and Module 3. This guide covers the material for Module 3, but the questions in this section cover the content from both modules.

Section A

(1) (a) What is meant by:
      (i) product portfolio (Evidence A, line 2)?   (2 marks)
      (ii) brand (Evidence A, line 2)?   (2 marks)
      (iii) operating profit (Evidence A, line 4)?   (2 marks)
   (b) Discuss why lifestyle changes may account for a change in demand
      for a product such as Heinz Salad Cream (Evidence B).   (6 marks)
   (c) Examine the view that advertising can only delay the inevitable decline
      of ageing products.   (8 marks)
   (d) Critically assess the importance of brands to a business.   (10 marks)

                                                   Total: 30 marks

■ ■ ■

Candidate's answer to question 1

(a) (i) Product portfolio is the list of products that a business produces. For example, Premier Foods produces Branston Pickle but also beans, custard and tea.

    📝 The definition is weak, but the use of an example drawn from the evidence is good and is enough to allow the examiner to give the candidate the benefit of the doubt.

                                                       2 marks

(ii) A brand is something like a name of a product. It is what a product is known by.

> A brand is more than just a name and the answer should specify the main point that a brand conveys an image or is a means of generating recognition and association with a particular product. There is no example to support the answer, nor any reference to the evidence. **0 marks**

(iii) Operating profit is the same as net profit. It is the profit made when the variable costs and the overheads have been taken into account.

> This is a competent answer that shows some understanding and uses appropriate terminology. An example from the evidence — especially when you are pointed to it in the question — would be a useful addition to this answer to guarantee the 2 marks. If the examiner has any doubt about your definition, a supporting example is usually enough to earn you full marks. **2 marks**

(b) A product like Heinz Salad Cream is seen as being old-fashioned. It has been around for some time and is not something that is bought by many young people. It may have been the case that this is something that people 30 years ago would have used regularly with salads but today, there are a lot more things that people have with their salad. This is partly to do with the wider range of foods we have in the UK and may be something to do with the number of immigrants to the country who have brought with them new types of foods like curries. As a result, young people have not been brought up with salad cream in the same way that their parents might have been and so tend not to buy it.

> This answer shows a lot of awareness and has much to recommend it. The candidate understands the wider social changes that have had an impact on the market for different types of food and, for the most part, keeps to the point of the question. The language of the response is a little informal and the candidate could make more use of the Nuffield toolkit — for example, by mentioning a fall in demand for salad cream, the existence of substitutes for a product such as salad cream, a change in the age structure of the population and also a simple change in tastes. Applying these methods and concepts distinguishes a general knowledge response from a good business and economics answer. **4 marks**

(c) Advertising is an important part of the marketing mix. It is used to persuade or inform and is known as informative advertising and persuasive advertising. Advertising can be 'above the line', where adverts are placed on television and are designed to reach lots of people, or 'below the line', which is more of a one-to-one method of advertising — for example, mailing out information to people on an e-mail list. Advertising is designed to increase sales and increase demand. We look at the advertising elasticity of demand to see whether advertising has been useful or not.

> This is an interesting response. The candidate has clearly done some revision and knows about advertising. He/she uses many important terms such as 'above the

line' and 'advertising elasticity' (neither of which are part of the specification) and shows good knowledge of the subject. However, the candidate makes a serious error here: although this response may be an interesting regurgitation of learned notes, it does not answer the set question. The examiner expects you not only to demonstrate your knowledge but also to apply that knowledge appropriately. The command word in the question is '*Examine* the view', but the candidate ignores this and simply writes all that he/she knows about advertising. This is an important lesson to learn — you will not be rewarded with many marks if you do not answer the question that is set.

The point of this question is to consider whether advertising just delays decline or can revitalise an ageing product. Branston Pickle has been around for many years and occasional advertising campaigns are run to remind consumers of its presence in the market, as is also the case with Kellogg's Cornflakes, for example. But is the decline inevitable? This depends on the product and on the type of advertising strategy used, the amount of money put into supporting the product and so on.

This candidate's answer gets little reward because it does not answer the question and makes no reference to the context of the evidence. He/she earns 1 mark for some demonstration of knowledge. **1 mark**

(d) A brand is an important thing for any business. A brand will give a business an image or an identity and as such means that people know about the brand and will buy the product again and again. This is called repeat purchase. Some products like Armani, Adidas and Nike are very well-known names and people will go to these brands first before buying from other companies. This gives the firms a competitive advantage and will boost sales and profits. Without a brand a business will encounter problems quickly and may even go bust. A brand name allows a business to charge more for its products.

This answer is similar to that given for part (c). It shows some knowledge but the language and expression are often weak. Neither answer (c) nor answer (d) makes any use of the evidence supplied. Your answers should always refer to the evidence and use the context presented to frame your response. In this case, is the fact that Premier Foods has spent a great deal of money buying a well-known and respected brand, such as Bird's or Quorn, evidence that a brand name is important to such a firm? Have you ever heard of Premier Foods?

When making a critical assessment, you are also expected to balance your answer. A brand may be important, but it has to be supported by many factors — for example, a reputation for good quality, the right sort of pricing strategy, good management etc.

This candidate's answer provides good evidence of knowledge but not of the other assessment objectives. There is no critical assessment apart from a cursory evaluative statement at the beginning — no questioning of why brands may be important to a business or even of the assumption that brands are important.

There is too much focus on learned knowledge and not enough on exam technique and the assessment objectives.   **4 marks**

ℓ **Overall score: 13/30 marks. This response is in the D-grade range. There is some solid evidence that the candidate understands the content of the modules, but he/she does not meet the demands of the range of skills assessed at AS. He/she should focus more on the assessment objectives and exam technique and less on the content.**

Section B

Evidence C

China loosens its grip on its currency

The Chinese government has followed up its revaluation of its currency (the yuan) in July 2005 — which led to the currency appreciating slightly against other currencies — with a further indication that it will allow the yuan to move more freely. China's export growth has been massive and critics argue that this is being fuelled by the artificially low value of the yuan against international currencies such as the US dollar. In addition, it makes investing in China more expensive than perhaps should be the case and, given the cultural and political differences between China and the West, this merely adds to the difficulties of Western governments trying to tap into the opportunities that China presents.

Evidence D

China to continue rapid economic growth

The Organisation for Economic Cooperation and Development (OECD) released its latest report on the state of the Chinese economy in late December 2005. The OECD sees economic growth in China remaining above 9% for the next 3 years. The rapid rate of growth has contributed to the increase in global oil and steel prices as Chinese manufacturing industry demands more and more to fuel economic expansion in the country. China is so vast and its capacity so great, however, that few analysts expect this high rate of growth to trigger inflation in China.

(2) (a) **Explain the links between economic growth and inflation.** (6 marks)
   (b) **Comment on the likely effect of the decision to revalue the Chinese yuan against other currencies.** (6 marks)
   (c) **Examine possible methods that the Chinese government might use to combat inflationary pressures in the economy.** (8 marks)
   (d) **Using aggregate demand and supply analysis, evaluate the possible effects on the Chinese economy of its continued strength in export markets.** (10 marks)

Total: 30 marks

Candidate's answer to question 2

(a) Economic growth can lead to high levels of inflation, which can subsequently lead to an increased cost of living, and if inflation is high enough then the standard of living could decrease and the economy could crash. This has not been the case in China. There economic growth has consistantly been above those in other OECD countries. They also managed to be resilient against the asian financial crash in the late 1990s.

 The candidate mentions the link between economic growth and inflation but does not *explain* it. He/she comments on the possible effect of high inflation and then falls into the trap of making an extreme prediction that the economy could crash — you should be wary of making extreme comments. There is some awareness of China's economic position in the world, but this is not focused on the question.

There is little indication that the candidate has looked at the evidence, which states clearly that China's economic growth looks set to continue for another 3 years and that there are currently no real inflationary pressures. A stronger candidate would recognise that economic growth can lead to inflationary pressures if the level of aggregate demand is rising faster than aggregate supply. An increase in the rate of inflation from 2% to 2.5%, for example, is a sign that the rate of growth of prices is speeding up. However, an inflation rate of 2.5% is hardly likely to lead to a full-scale economic disaster, but this is nevertheless a link between economic growth and inflation.

There are some spelling and grammar mistakes in the answer. You are advised on the front page of the exam paper that the quality of your written English will be taken into account. **1 mark**

(b) This is great for China as the currency will rise as more people are demanding it. The more people demand the currency, the higher the price for the currency through an increase in the price equilibrium (where demand meets supply). If China were to put its prices up, then demand would fall for its product and the value of China's currency would fall dramatically. Importing goods may be expensive for the business as it will have to pay import duties tariffs.

This answer illustrates the confusion that is all too common in responses involving exchange rates. Invariably the confusion stems from which country the discussion is based in and from the terminology used in discussing exchange rates. This question is about the revaluation of the yuan. The evidence suggests that the currency may be valued below the level that its trade situation would imply. The revaluation may mean that the value of the yuan will rise against other currencies. The candidate recognises that the currency will rise and suggests that 'this is great for China' but does not explain why this is the case. In the case of exchange rates, whether a rise in currency is good or bad depends on whether you are an importer or an exporter.

It is also important to remember that this question and the pieces of evidence are about China. Therefore, you should try to view the situation from a Chinese perspective. The last line of this answer does not do this. What is meant by 'the business' — a Chinese firm or a British one? Does the candidate mean 'import' or 'export'?

The whole answer is confused and demonstrates a lack of clear thinking and understanding. There is some understanding in the reference to supply and demand but it is not particularly detailed. It is also unclear what the relevance is of the reference to China putting its prices up — does the candidate think that a rise in the exchange rate is the same as exporters in China increasing the price for their products? In reality, of course, the price of Chinese products may not have changed at all — the rise in the exchange rate gives the impression to foreign buyers that prices have gone up because they now have to give up more of their currency to buy the same amount of yuan. Understanding this effect is vital when answering questions on exchange rates. **2 marks**

(c) When there is economic growth, booms and recessions occur. The Chinese government will need to keep economic growth at a steady pace because if it grows too fast, then there will be a slump in the economy. The Chinese government will then have to use fiscal or monetary policies to sort out the problem of inflation. Fiscal policy is where taxes are increased or decreased and this has an effect on spending. Monetary policy is where the government changes interest rates and this also affects spending. If the government can stop spending, then it can prevent inflation from happening and the economy will not crash like it did in Germany in 1923. Inflation is considered to be bad because of the effect on the value of money.

This candidate has done some revision but does not show much understanding. The answer lacks coherence, planning and structure. It jumps from one point to another without any logic and contains a number of irrelevant points that pad out the response. The candidate does not pay attention to the command words in the question.

The opening sentence shows a lack of understanding of economic growth — be wary of the tendency to explain issues in terms of extremes. The UK economy has not experienced a boom or a recession since the 1990s; the path of economic growth has been much smoother and more stable.

Next, the candidate writes that a boom will cause a slump. If economic growth is rising rapidly (in the example of China, at over 9%), this is clearly not a slump. Eventually he/she gets to the point of the question by referring to fiscal and monetary policy. There is vague understanding of the link between the two but no detail is given about the way in which monetary policy and fiscal policy are used to curb inflationary pressures. The candidate makes an elementary mistake in stating that the government controls monetary policy — it is now determined by the Bank of England. The lack of specificity in the answer continues — does the government want to 'stop' spending? Does it want to prevent inflation from happening at all? Is the situation in China anything like that in Germany in 1923? Overall, this answer is constructed badly and written poorly and does not demonstrate the understanding expected of an AS student. **2 marks**

(d) If China's economy keeps on growing without any slumps, then the demand for its goods will get higher and then China can charge the prices it wants to charge. However, if it charges too much, then other countries will have to find other ways of getting those materials or goods and the demand will fall and China will have a large supply and nothing to do with it, so it will then drop its prices and the same process will happen again.

e The candidate continues to demonstrate a poor level of understanding of the macroeconomic elements in the unit. Although demand and supply and the link between demand and prices are mentioned, the examiner expects greater understanding from a student who has studied the subject for at least 9 months.

The answer contains no reference to aggregate demand and supply and no diagram. There is no evidence that the candidate knows the formula for aggregate demand ($AD = C + I + G + (X - M)$) and/or understands the role that exports and imports play in determining the level of aggregate demand. In addition, there is no real evidence of any evaluation and it seems as though the candidate has run out of time — the answer is short, even though it is meant to address the longest and most challenging question on the paper. **2 marks**

e **Overall score: 7/30 marks. This answer would fail to achieve a grade. The candidate shows little evidence of any real understanding of the subject matter. However, there is much that you can learn from this sort of answer — by not making the same mistakes. Try marking the answers yourself, by highlighting where a lack of understanding occurs and by writing what you think the candidate should be saying.**

Section C

(3) (a) **Assess the methods that a British firm may use to compete with Chinese firms.** (10 marks)

(b) **Critically examine the view that the level of growth in the Chinese economy is unsustainable in the long run.** (20 marks)

Total: 30 marks

■ ■ ■

Candidate's answer to question 3

(a) British firms may not have the capability to compete on price with Chinese firms because of the Chinese comparative advantage of low production costs. However, the British have a comparative advantage in innovation and could therefore employ these innovative skills to improve the quality of their products. They could then adopt a premium pricing strategy in accordance with their quality products. They could also boost sales at home by marketing the fact that the products are made in Britain. They could also try to create a strong brand image not only in the British market but also in other markets such as Europe, Asia and America. This could give their product a competitive advantage by adding value to their product.

Alternatively a British firm could move production to where labour is cheap, for example India. This could reduce its production costs enabling it to reduce price, increase quality or add value to its product.

 The candidate uses a number of terms and concepts, showing that he/she has revised and understands the issue. The answer starts by commenting on comparative advantage in China, which is a good point. Although comparative advantage is not covered in this unit, it is relevant to this question.

The answer offers four strategies — innovation, pricing, 'made in Britain' branding and moving location. However, for this question two or three strategies would have been enough if they were supported well. It is the *evaluation* of the strategies that is important, rather than the number of strategies discussed. This answer fails to evaluate the strategies. In addition, the candidate makes many assumptions: that moving production to India is possible and costless, and would add value, increase quality and reduce price.

More marks could have been gained by evaluating the strategies suggested. For example, on what would the success of the innovation strategy depend? What level of innovation is needed? What does the candidate mean by 'premium pricing'? How much higher do prices need to be? Would this policy be enough to overcome the competition presented by the Chinese? The candidate could also have offered an example of how such innovation may succeed in overcoming competition.

5 marks

(b) The evidence tells us that the Chinese economy is growing very quickly. 9% is a very high rate of growth and the OECD thinks that it will continue to be at this level for the next 3 years. The evidence also says that people think that this is not likely to trigger inflation. Sustainable growth is a level of economic growth that does not cause inflation to get out of hand. This is all to do with *AD* and *AS*. If *AD* is growing, it is shifting to the right and this can cause a rise in inflation.

But this might not happen if the *AS* is also rising. In China it says that people don't think it will cause inflation and this means that there must be lots of resources not being used. The amount of resources is important in the *AS*. China is a big country and has a big population, over a billion, so there is no shortage of people to work in factories and build things. This means that the *AS* will also move and so inflation will not occur.

On the whole, the economy in China will continue to grow strongly and will be sustainable.

This competent answer makes a good attempt at the question and shows some reasonable understanding of the issue. The language used lets it down as it is a little simplistic in parts. The other main problem is the lack of detailed critical assessment. The answer does have some balance and therefore offers some evaluation. There is a conclusion and the response is well structured. The candidate could have included a diagram to demonstrate the points being made and to show that he/she can use appropriate models. He/she also assumes wrongly that China's massive resources are all readily accessible and that its population can adapt to manufacture any type of product.

Although the Chinese economy is set to grow strongly over the next few years, the evidence suggests that its rate of growth is causing upward pressure on oil prices. The candidate could have made more critical assessment in the answer by mentioning the long-run *AS* curve and suggesting that the position of China's economy on the *AS* curve may determine whether a rate of growth of *AD* of 9% is sustainable in the long term. This depends on the extent to which China can utilise the resources it has at its disposal.

This answer does have some merits and is a good attempt at the question.

13 marks

Overall score: 18/30 marks. This is a solid B-grade answer that shows some evidence of understanding and an appreciation of the assessment objectives. The candidate needs to improve his/her evaluation and language skills in order to get an A grade.